The 21-Day Mindfulness Challenge

mindfulness for beginners, a simple step-by-step guide to living in the present moment and creating more calm, joy and focus in your life

21-Day Challenges

ISBN-13: 978-1515145226
ISBN-10: 1515145220

The 21-Day Challenges
Kindle & Paperback

Happiness

Self-love

Self-Confidence

Mindfulness

Stress Management

Minimalism

Productivity

Budgeting

Exercise

Weight Loss

Clean Eating

Introduction

You wake up to the alarm screaming at you. You hit snooze a few times before getting out of bed. Why are you so tired? Who knows. You start going through the motions of getting ready for work, almost on autopilot. Somehow it gets to be 7:30 and you're late again, so you race out, nearly colliding with someone coming by on a bike that you completely didn't see coming.

You have this vague sense of irritation that you're not really sure about, so you assume it's the cyclist and you yell a few choice words at him. At that moment you forget to bring your lunch you packed the night before but you'll only notice this 4 hours later when you get a hunger headache...

When this eventually happens later that day you're irritated and find yourself being snippy with your poor work colleagues. You go to the mall to pick something up and find yourself tempted to buy an overpriced trinket just to cheer yourself up. You do so and immediately remember you decided last week not to do that anymore. Dammit! You have a weird conversation with your friend where you have trouble understanding what they're on about and then the rest of the day floats by in a haze.

You get home that evening and can't really say where the time has gone. You feel a dim sense of life passing you by. You stub your toe on the stupid doorframe as you stomp around your house, thinking of something else. The same slight panic that you usually get in the late afternoons creeps in and suddenly you're eaten up by anxiety and worries. In turn, you eat up all yesterday's leftovers in the fridge. Dammit! What if your life is never more than this?

Where did your life go? What happened? You feel like you've tried so hard to make goals and plan out your dreams, but it's days like these you just start to wonder what the point is at all. You stay up too late trying to numb the creeping sensations with too much food and TV. You don't notice how tired you are. You collapse into bed and before you know it ...the alarm wakes you up the next morning again.

Day One: How Mindful are You?

If anything of the previous story resonated with you, chances are you've experienced mindlessness ...or are doing it right now (hey you - pay attention!). Are you reading this book half-heartedly, thinking about other things while you only skim? How many distracting thoughts have you had since starting this very chapter?

During this challenge we'll be looking at what mindfulness is, and trying it on for size in our own lives right here and right now. Like all the best things in life, mindfulness is better *done* rather than just talked about, so we'll finish each day with a brief exercise.

Today, haul out a notebook to start tracking your progress. To begin, start by identifying sticky areas that you believe could be improved. Answer the following questions - honestly - and start thinking about what it *really* is you want to get out of this challenge.

- Can you remember the last time you relished a meal, the scent of a flower, a kiss or some good piece of music? Hopefully, it was a little more recently than last Valentine's day...

- Do you "multitask"?

- What's the *very first* thing you do every morning ...and the last thing you do right before you fall asleep?

- Do you often feel like you're in a big fat rush?

- Are you clumsy? Go on, you can admit it if you're regularly falling over, bruising yourself or dropping things!

- Do you lose your temper easily?

- Are you often completely surprised by other people's behavior?

- Do you often have "mood swings" that you can't explain?

Once you've jotted down some of the answers to these questions, don't feel the need to rush right in and go into frantic "life-fix-up" mode (strange advice from a self help book, I know!) and just go with it.

Day Two: What Mindfulness Feels Like

You have probably already spent a few mindful moments in your life, spontaneously. These were bright, clear moments in the dim rush of regular life, moments where you felt your mind go still for a while. When you are mindful, everything is "switched on" and all the data from all your senses is coming in quickly and without being distorted. You are alert yet calm, and there is no rush, and nowhere to go. You've been there before - and you can go there again!

Welcome to the present

The present moment is a strange place. We are all trapped here, really, and there is utterly *no other place to be*, yet so few of us take a moment to stop and have a look around. The future and the past all exist in the mind. They are only ever memories, dreams, little flickers in the electrified meat we generously call our brains. The only thing that is real is the moment that is happening right now.

Take a moment to stop, right now (when else?) and feel the moment. Feel how full it is? It is something that is always *becoming*, but in each moment it is already started, already complete. The present is everything that ever was and ever will be, right now. History is dead, and the future doesn't exist. All that is real is the moment now, as it unfolds.

Because humans like to make symbols, to make plans and remember the past and create huge systems of meaning around them, it's easy for us to forget that our original habitat was the present moment. We talk and think about abstract things and forget about the reality that is right under our noses. We get caught up in theories and wishes about reality so that we miss it when reality reveals itself plain and simple, right before our eyes.

To get to know the present, all you have to do is be aware.

"Awareness" is like all your senses rolled up into one, or, more accurately, it is the *main* sense, and all the others are variations on it. Awareness is a keen and conscious perception of the universe as it is around you. Once you become more comfortable with your awareness, it starts to seem natural to think of "you" versus "the world" as a bit of an arbitrary distinction anyway. Awareness is the opposite of mindlessness, of inattention, of inelegance and haphazard, unfocused action.

Awareness doesn't come with any ornaments: it just is. It isn't awareness of a thing as good or a thing as bad. It is only awareness of a thing, period. There is no judgment attached to it, no expectation. Just calm, quiet appreciation of the fabric of existence as it appears through the lens of your being an awake, sentient being.

Thought traffic

But try to become aware of the simple things around you though - the sound of the birds in the trees, the smell of your coffee brewing - and you'll notice instantly that there is something preventing you from immersing yourself fully: your thought traffic. If you've ever tried to make dinner with a bored two year old in your presence, or tried *not* to think of a pink elephant (try it right now!) then you'll know the feeling.

You might have become so used to the constant stream of thoughts that you don't even notice it anymore. In fact, if you're like any human being living in the modern world today, you'll likely just call this thought traffic "me".

But your thoughts are no more part of you than clouds are a part of the sky, or ripples are a part of the water. Lots of things go on in your average sky - clouds, rain, thunder, whatever - but underneath it is always just sky. Your thoughts are the same. They come ...but they also go. They may be "good" or they may be "bad". But they are all *impermanent*. Nobody would latch their identities onto something as fleeting as a cloud, and yet almost all of us latch our identities onto things even more fleeting and empty: thoughts and sensations.

When you do attach yourself to things that are impermanent, you cause yourself to suffer. Makes sense, right? You get all attached to something that was never really that real to start with and then when it goes (as it must!) you experience loss. You feel like you've been cheated, like the universe owes you one, like everything is *wrong*.

But nothing is wrong. Everything is as it should be. Life is transient, and our experiences here are also transient. The first step to developing a calm sense of mindfulness is to realize that the fleeting thoughts and sensations are *not reality* at all.

The next step is to learn to watch the fleeting sensations come and go without attaching to them. Instead of suffering, you feel resilient and tranquil in the face of whatever life is. You become still inside, awake and deeply aware of the world around you, without having a desperate need to change it.

Today, try to get in touch with your own sense of awareness. Send out a little feeler into the universe. Is it difficult to hold this sense of awareness? Boring? Strange? Try it out at moments throughout the day and note how it feels. Again, there's no test at the end of this book and you won't be receiving a report card - just observe and accept.

Day Three: Thought Traffic

Thought traffic is difficult to stop, but thankfully you don't really have to. You only have to be *aware* that you're doing it. Imagine you have a bad argument with your brother on the phone and come home, agitated and upset, The more you think about the idiotic things he said, the angrier and hurt you become. You replay the moment in your mind again and again. For those few hours that you are stewing, you are not in the present moment anymore. You don't notice anything that is happening, or the part you play in it. You are mindless.

Your thoughts start taking up more and more space until they're the only thing you can think of. You fight with him mentally, dreaming up counterarguments and bitchy retorts and thinking of all the ways he shouldn't have done what he did.

Well, if you were mindful, what would be different?

Bad news: you might still have had a fight with your brother. The good news though, is you'd be able to look at the resulting thought traffic for what it really is: transient. On one level, you'd feel angry and hurt, sure, but you'd be able to take a deep breath and *watch yourself having those thoughts.* You'd know that just like everything else, those thoughts would soon drift off. Awareness is an incredible way to "snap out of" moments like this because it reminds us that our emotions are just a temporary state of affairs.

Today, try to take a peek inside your head and see what thought traffic you have buzzing around. The easiest way to do this is ...to try and focus on something else. Casually try to tune your awareness onto something in the environment and within a few moments, your thoughts will begin to poke their noses into things:

Don't forget that thing you have to do this afternoon
You're slouching again, you promised yourself you'd stop slouching
Man I love this song
I made this tea too weak
I wonder if cats ever fart?
Damn I have to RSVP to that wedding

I'm too old for anyone to love me now, I'll probably never get married
I mustn't think that, the more I stress the less likely it is I'll meet
someone
I have to shave
What time is it?
Ah here, this is the best part in the song
I'm sure cats can't fart, that's ridiculous
I can smell honeysuckle
What's so wrong with wanting a relationship anyway? I'm allowed to be
vulnerable
I wonder what's for dinner
It's kind of lame to have weddings in the first place, Jesus it's going to be
so boring
Don't forget that thing you have to do this afternoon

And on and on and on...

What happened to that full and glorious present moment we were
talking about? It's gone!

Thought traffic basically only stops when you sleep, and that's even
debatable. Have you ever seen someone absentmindedly talking to
themselves? You've probably thought, "oh my god they're crazy" but
when you think about it, all they're doing is saying aloud what all of us
do quietly in our minds anyway. I know people would think I was crazy if
I said out loud some of the rubbish that passes in and out of my head on
the average day!

In the next few days, we'll look at what to do about thought traffic, but
for now, it's enough to simply become aware of it and know that it's
actually there at all.

Day Four: Myths About Mindfulness

You have to be a Buddhist to practice mindfulness

It's true that mindfulness is most associated with Buddhist thought of all kinds, but that doesn't mean that "becoming" a Buddhist is necessary to doing mindfulness right. Some people may get stressed with the idea of being "correct" and will spend time and money on books, seminars and chatting to strange-smelling "gurus" so that they get just the right flavor of awareness. This is unnecessary.

There is no one culture or life philosophy that owns the idea of mindfulness, and you can certainly be mindful without subscribing to many of the ideas that cluster around the concept. In fact, if you notice people trying to one up each other over who has the most open chakras or who's winning the mindfulness Olympics, you can be sure they'll be more tangled in ego than in cultivating their consciousness.

Mindfulness is a religion

This ties into the previous point, but in a lot of ways, mindfulness is best when it's short and simple. Find a practice that is high on the compassion side and less about any spiritual rulebooks. Mindfulness is not a religion in the slightest, although it can fit quite well alongside a religion if you wanted it to. Because mindfulness is not a quality of the content of your mind, but of your mind itself, it's compatible with whatever life path you're on.

Here, this book may differ a little from what's on offer elsewhere in that there is no assumed value judgment in the awareness we are trying to develop. Though the Buddha himself promoted "right thinking" and "right action", I'm not the Buddha (not even close) and in this book the act of mindfulness itself is value-neutral. Of course, while I think it's technically possible to be a mindful and consciously aware psychopath murderer, my hunch is that simply by being aware, you probably won't opt for that. While value-driven behavior is often a result of becoming more mindful, it's not explicitly the goal, as with religions.

You have to meditate to be mindful

Meditation is not the same thing as mindfulness in the same way that thinking is not the same as going to school. While going to school certainly means thinking is more likely to happen, going to school in and of itself is nothing special.

A great Buddhist master was once asked by his student what he did before he was enlightened, and he answered, "I swept the floor". When asked what he did after he was enlightened, he answered, "I swept the floor".

In other words, there's nothing unique and magical about putting down a mat and sitting down to meditate. It's not any more momentous or high-minded than breathing deeply and accessing a calm, accepting state of mindfulness while you clean out the cat litter box every Tuesday.

Mindfulness is apathetic

To be mindful, people are sometimes asked to withhold judgments, to not attach values to things and to truly, deeply accept them. It's all well and good until the thing that you're asked to accept is your boss asking you to work late again on a Friday to fix a mistake he made. Just accept that guy who cut you off in traffic? I personally have a hard time with this! For many people, abandoning the knee-jerk need to judge and evaluate everything as good or bad is so automatic, they feel almost naked without it. You know, in a bad way.

The obvious thing to wonder is, "if I accept this crappy thing, then how am I ever going to solve it? I don't want to be a pushover. I'm not Ghandi here" and it's a legitimate issue. The thing is, you can act to improve your life, to maintain your boundaries, engage in goal setting behavior ...and still tell your boss exactly where to stick it without getting attached. Yes!

In Buddhist philosophy, attachment leads to suffering. It is our clinging and grasping and desire that causes us to suffer, not the world as it is. Apathy is seeing that something is not to your liking and being too tired / fed up / depressed to do anything about it. Apathy is hopeless and cynical, and most importantly, it doesn't lead to action. Apathy feels like crap too, but that's another story.

True acceptance is not apathy, though. If somebody insults my mother's fudge brownies then I have a few options. If I'm attached to my thoughts of her value as a cook, to how other people ought to behave and to the undeniable deliciousness of the brownies in question (seriously, who could deny it? Only someone who's out to hurt, that's who), then I will cling to an outcome I want, maybe argue with the person, retaliate, even stew about it for hours or days after the insult happens.

Apathy is feeling all of this and deciding there's nothing you can do about it, but acceptance is a little more nuanced. If someone doesn't agree with me and insults me, does it really harm me much? Is getting upset going to change their opinion? Is someone's opinion on a baked good all that important (this is just a hypothetical example, in this case, of course it's important)? Is it fair that I should expect everyone to have the same tastes as me? Is it a rule that I must never be insulted? If I am insulted, what's the big deal? Could they even be right?

I mean, it's perfectly possible somebody insults you a little worse than what I've described above, but even then, there's still no point in attaching to your thoughts and ideas about it. If you are in danger, remove yourself from it. If you've made a mistake, fix it. If something isn't working, try something else. Done.

Nowhere do you need to have your ego attached to be effective in any of these things, though. Do what you need to do, then carry on. Just as clouds float over the sky and away again, and just as thoughts float into your awareness and away again, life events come and go. What's important is your continued, calm, non-attached blue sky behind it.

Mindfulness feels really blissful and amazing

In the corporate world, the place where every good idea goes to die a slow and painful death, Mindfulness™ is sold to human resources ~~fools~~ people as a great sedative for the masses. Send your staff on a mindfulness-training course and they'll be calmer and less anxious, and hopefully nicer to one another (and maybe they won't notice how new regulations you've introduced are actually screwing them over...)

Mindfulness is sold as a metaphysical snake oil that blisses you out and makes you super-chilled, unflappable and just, like, nice. But the truth is that mindfulness doesn't feel particularly joyful or ecstatic. While it's true that learning to really tune into the preciousness of the moment around you may make it more likely you catch those winds of joy when they blow your way, it's not really guaranteed.

It doesn't have quite the same whizz-bang appeal as bliss and joy does, but tranquility and calm are more accurately the outcomes of mindfulness. What I'm saying is that life's problems don't evaporate into a puff of sandalwood incense smoke. Nope, they're still there, you're just looking at them differently.

Mindfulness can soothe stress and solve all your mental health issues

Related to the last point, the idea of mindfulness as a prescription for mental illness can be a pretty dangerous one. It's a nice illusion, but sadly "mind over matter" doesn't always apply, for example if the matter we're talking about is a legitimate physiological problem in the brain. While mindfulness will definitely help, it's not a solution on its own.

Do you suffer from anxiety? Depression? Trauma? For some people, sitting quietly and asking the mind to quiet down can be precisely the thing that causes the mind to go into overdrive. You can set in motion a vicious cycle that only worsens anxiety or causes your defenses to break down. Likewise, if you're a melancholic sort, playing around with kooky ideas of "no-self" and the fleetingness of life's sensations might leave you feeling in a little bit of funk.

My point is not that mindfulness can't help these conditions - anecdotally, many people find a deep relief in a meditation practice that they don't find anywhere else. Nevertheless, meditation is not a cure-all or silver bullet. As with anything, be responsible, dear reader. Today's exercise: ask yourself what's your take on some of these "myths"?

Day Five: Mindful Eating

Today, a fun exercise to flex our new awareness muscles when it comes to just about the most fun you can have in this world: eating. We're all guilty of a little mindless eating now and then. Fine. We overeat because we may not notice that expanding feeling in our belts. We keep eating something that doesn't agree with us because we lack the presence of mind to notice its effect on us. We scoff down things without a second thought - or even a first one!

Step one: find some food. Easy enough. It doesn't have to be a level 5 vegan platter worthy of a food magazine photo shoot, it just has to be food, that's all. Before you eat, take a deep breath and sit a moment with the plate before you, appreciating the fullness of the moment and the significance of what you're about to do.

Step two: find your breath, become focused and gently alert ...and start eating. Don't rush. Eat and pay attention to everything you can. The texture of the food in your mouth, the subtleties of the flavor, thoughts about it ("this isn't on my diet" or "yum!" or "could use some salt"), the sensation of how your jaw and teeth are breaking it down, the smell, everything. Hear the sound of your fork clinking on the plate. Take your time. Take another bite.

Imagine the food going into your body, being digested. Think about how it will be translated into energy, and will somewhere along the line become your actions, your thoughts and words. Think that in time, you'll also be broken down and "digested" by life (deep! Just go with it). If you notice yourself thinking, "man this is lame, I'm way too old for this shit", then simply watch yourself having the thought and let it go.

If you're eating meat, think of the animal's life, all of it, and the journey it took to reach your plate. Look at the vegetables on your plate and think of all the processes that went into creating it, right from the rays of a burning ball of gas billions of miles away to the man in another country who dug it up with his bare hands and started the journey it took to land those vegetables in front of you right now. Take your time. Take another bite.

Naturally, you'd be the world's lousiest dinner companion if you carried on like this at every meal, but once in a while it can be a very illuminating experience. Overeating is very often a case of failing to notice that you're actually full already, or that you weren't really hungry for food in the first place. Many food allergies and sensitivities could have been discovered earlier if people were just a bit more curious about what was going on in their bodies as they ate.

Day Six: Reflect

Today, take a brief moment to do a "mindfulness reading" on the contents of your mind. Take your own awareness pulse and, like a nurse for the soul, jot it down somewhere to come back and look at later. Are you bored? Excited? Cynical? Distracted?

Day Seven: The Trap Of "McMindfulness"

The Buddha, if he's in a grave anywhere, would probably be rolling around in it a little if he knew how some of his life's work had become so warped with time. Of course the Buddha, as lovely as he no doubt is, is not the owner of mindfulness. Nevertheless there is something in the fact that if there's a life philosophy out there worth anything, there's also someone out there wondering how to make a quick buck from it with a few catchy Amazon titles and a cheesy seminar for just $19.99.

Ladies and gentlemen, "McMindfulness", which if you know how much I like word play, is a wonderful term. As much as your standard free-love hippie in the Western world likes to think otherwise, the Eastern conception of mindfulness just doesn't sit very well in our modern consumer capitalist society.

The result? What is meant to be light (so light it's almost empty!), joyful and unattached becomes another lame brand of enlightenment™. This turns mindfulness into a way to trick yourself into some fabulous inner peace you can buy and put on the shelf right next to your vegan cookbooks and Himalayan salt lamp. It's just another thing to own and have, something to enrich you personally, something to lord over those less awakened plebs, something you expect to see in an ad that ends with a suggestion to "ask your doctor if mindfulness is right for you…"

I apologize for being cynical. But clinging to mindfulness is still clinging. Greed, fear, dissatisfaction, grasping, expectation and mindlessness are always what they are, even if you put a sophisticated wrapper on it. While mindfulness certainly does have benefits for your mental health (and blood pressure!), and probably makes you a nicer person all round, it isn't *for* this that you become mindful. It's easy to get trapped in an image, in a marketed picture of what mindfulness can do to make your life more beautiful, less full of pain and confusing, just *better*. But this, too, is something to become aware of, and ultimately, to let go of.

Today, ask yourself honestly if you've ever tried to buy awareness. Have you ever succumbed to advertising trying to exploit your desire for self-improvement? Do you have any unrealistic expectations of what it looks like to be mindful?

Day Eight: The "Happy Ending" and Why You Need to Drop it

Lets go further. Every culture in the world and every person who ever lived has built in mental machinery called the "happy ending". Let me explain. A happy ending can be many different things, but it usually has a few characteristics:

1. It happens in the future
2. It's perfect and awesome and fabulous
3. It's finished and complete

Look at a lot of what captures human beings' interest in this world, and you'll see that much of it fits the bill of the "happy ending". The Christian heaven. The "after" picture for every product designed ever (but ...if companies really succeeded in making you so smiley and happy, how on earth would they *keep on* selling you more things, right?). Any cult or self help group or best selling life-fix-up book. Utopia. The brochures for that children's charity you donate to.

They all point to the same irresistible dream we have: that one day, *one day*, we'll arrive at a place where everything will make sense, everything will finally be right, we can stop striving and grasping, all problems will be solved and we can just finally sit back and enjoy the perfection of it.

If you're older than 30, have had enough sour breakups or have ever tried Weightwatchers, this idea will strike you as ridiculous on its face. But even still, all of us buy into it to some extent. A friend of mine is a neat freak. She may not know it, but for her, Nirvana looks like complete order, a bleached kitchen counter and the faint scent of forest pine in the air. Ah, but life is not like that, is it? You only get to kill *99.9%* of the germs. Tomorrow, you start again.

Today's exercise: Letting go of the perfect "happy ending".

What does yours look like? Modern, Western self help logic will say it's great to have goals, that you should think of the future constantly and strive to be bigger, better, faster ...all the time. That you should buy into your life love story and never stop running after it. But running after that future point does one thing: kills the living vitality in the *present moment*. Creates dissatisfaction and more wanting. And the worst part is that, truthfully, you never get there. You only arrive at the end of your life, so busy and eager to get to the "future", and realize that you already passed it, that it all happened while you had your eyes fixed on something else, something unreal.

Today, try to let unanswered questions go. Try to look at your grand plans and big dreams and be OK with them never coming true. Really. Look at this moment in front of you and be OK with all its "imperfections". After all, who are we to judge reality and find it wanting?

Look at all the messy, confusing, imperfect things in your life today and say "OK". You could even try to do it literally. Your cat vomits all over your freshly laundered pile of laundry? "Ok". You received a 62% grade for a project? "Ok". Someone stood you up on a date you planned and never got back to you to explain why? "Ok." Things go horribly, strangely, unexpectedly wrong? "Ok". They go beautifully, strangely, unexpectedly *right*? "Ok".

Let go of the vision of yourself in the future, one that will make this moment worth it, justified. Just be here, in this moment, for everything that it is, not what it can be.

Day Nine: Creating Joy

Today, as you send your new awareness feeler out into the world (I'm thinking more along the lines of a bumblebee's and not a cockroach, but imagine whatever works for you) try to tune into fleeting moments of joy. This is where happiness lives: in the small things.

Can you go out today and be aware of all the millions of little miracles that are happening right under you nose all the time?

Day Ten: Embodied Mindfulness

Whenever I hear "mindfulness" it makes me think of, well, *minds*, and then I think of brains, or more accurately, a severed head. Meditation and mindfulness always seem to have this lofty vibe about them, don't they? As if anything to do with thoughts and introspection and insightful awareness and blah blah blah can't possibly have anything to do with a gross thing like a body.

But there's no reason you can't be aware with the whole of you. I know it's silly to think of, say, your little toe gaining a moment of blissful peace or the skin on the back of your arm smashing through samsara and attaining a refined and enlightened state of unattached nirvana. But ...why not?

Today, we'll shift our focus onto our whole body, not just the part of it that seems like a big deal because it has our eyes and ears attached to it. Even talking about "bodily awareness" as though it's a different thing from any kind of awareness reinforces a bit of a misconception. Here are a few ways you can practice and enhance your own sense of your body in space, how it moves, how it breathes, how it *is*. You can choose one of them or come up with your own.

- Do a "walking meditation". Start slowly by standing and beginning a brief meditation where you become aware of your breath, the way your weight is distributed in your feet, the sensation of air on your skin. When you have focused and found a balance, start to gently take a step, super slowly at first, just to explore what it's like to move, to play with the shift of balance over your heel, toes and ball of the foot. What it feels like to move through space. The feeling of the world pushing up from underneath you, and you pushing back down. Start walking slowly and keep a rhythm going. Focus all your attention on the intricacies of the movement. Let nothing else exist for you.

- Have a beautiful, mindful bath. You don't have to go out of your way with fancy bubbles or mood music (I said you don't *have to*, but like, you totally *can*) and turn your senses up. Dwell a while on the sights, sounds, smells, textures. Look outside of yourself (the sound of a dripping tap, the almost unfeelable feeling of steam touching your skin, the sight of a pile of laundry in the corner) and inside of yourself (a stomach squelch, a memory of an ex, the thought that you're such a slob and you really should do the laundry.)

- Some time during the day, take a moment to put on the brakes and just take a second to *stop and notice* what your body is up to. Do a little "body scan" and see what you find. Jagged breath? A weird twitch in your neck? That annoying song you've had stuck in your head since 8am? It's important here not to rush in to "fix" everything. It's not necessary to "correct" anything or make a judgment about what your senses discover. You don't have to seek out problems and then troubleshoot them (I always found this statement upsetting, as I visualize the poor trouble, cowering in a corner since you're about to shoot it - so violent!)

- Throw yourself into any activity that encourages you to get *into* your body. A lot of us basically live in our heads and just carry our meat along for the ride ...but some activities *need* you to turn off the thinking machine for a while and let your body take over. Weightlifting is a surprisingly effective way to shut off the thought traffic, as is (ludicrous, silly, over the top) dancing, as is doing anything that is intense and requires razor like focus like rock climbing, running or getting engrossed into a hobby that requires your full focus.

Day Eleven: Becoming Acquainted With What IS

So much of what we do can be categorized as "fighting with reality". Think about it. We look at the world like spoilt brats, pouting and wishing everything we experience was different. We take our ideas of what *should* be and then stomp our feet and wait for the atoms and molecules of the universe to hurry up and arrange themselves into a form that will please us.

If someone treats us in a way we think is unfair, we rail against it and argue with them, retaliate or find reason why they're wrong and we're right. We act surprised and hurt when things don't go our way. If there's a noise outside when we're trying to nap, we think, "dammit reality, you always do this!" but when our friends are napping when we message them and they don't respond quickly enough we think, "reality, you suck".

If we're sad, we rush out into the world to find a way to soothe ourselves and paint the smile back on to our faces. If we're hungry, we eat, sometimes a bunch (just in case!) and if it's cold, we complain and cover ourselves up.

But all of these things in life - pain, discomfort, hunger, inconvenience - they are all just a part of life. Often, the "problem" is that we have attached a big story to these sensations about why they're unacceptable and have to be gotten rid of as soon as possible. So we sit down to meditate and make a big story about how it's all *supposed* to go. It's guaranteed that your script doesn't include pesky intrusive thoughts about how your mother thinks you're a failure, the baby next door screaming or a growling stomach.

So these things happen and you think, "ah, this isn't right!" and try your best to wrestle poor old reality (who hasn't done anything to you) into the mold you've made for it. You tell your fears about your failings in life to shut up and keep quiet, secretly think nasty thoughts about how much you judge your neighbor for being a bad parent and make a mental note to stop eating so many brassicas.

What's happened? You're far, far, far out of the moment. All the fleeting sensations that have disrupted you have long gone, but they've set off a chain reaction of thoughts that have ripped you out of the moment. In this way, striving and reaching and grasping for what you wish was reality has actually gotten in the way of you experiencing reality.

Today, have a brief meditation session where you don't bitch and moan at what reality is. Instead of deciding what your opinion is on the things and sensations that float into your awareness, just becomes aware that they have. Don't be too concerned with *what* is, just *that it is.*

After all, whatever is, is whether we like it or not.

As you sit and meditate, try not to judge things that you become aware of. This means "good" judgments, too. Saying, "ah that's good, I like that" is no less of an attachment than, "I hate that and I wish it would stop". See if you can let the thing be what it is, and simply note its passing. You don't have to evaluate every little thing, or hold onto it to stop it slipping away, or help it slip away a little faster if you're not too keen on it.

This flies completely in the face of pretty much the entire self help culture we live in, but watch what happens when you just leave things be. There are no solutions, nothing to reach for, nothing to get away from. Just focus on the sounds, the sights, the sounds, without attaching your story to them, or arguing them into a different shape and form to suit you. This is an incredibly strange and difficult thing to do. But do it anyway!

Day Twelve: Creating "Windows"

We'll learn about formal meditation later on, but for today, we're going to practice the art of creating tiny awareness "windows". Throughout your day today, try to remember to "catch" a moment as it goes by. Stop, pause and become aware. You don't have to drag things out. Just stop, breathe and notice. Then go on with life. It might not seem like much, but if you can learn to open a window in dark or difficult times, you'll have learnt a skill few people on this earth can manage.

Day Thirteen: Becoming Aware of the Human Landscape

So far, we've spent some time learning to tune in more deeply to all the facets of the present moment: both the passing sensations in the external world, and the passing sensations in the internal one. Today, we'll expand our awareness to include other people.

When you unplug momentarily from the endless thought traffic and take a moment to just be in the present, it can feel a little isolating. But this movement doesn't have to be a turn inward. In fact, becoming more aware of yourself as you navigate the fullness of the present moment can actually make you much more personable and able to connect as a human to other humans.

Eons ago, human beings lived in small tribes, never reaching more than a few hundred people. This meant that you probably knew everyone around you, and those are more or less the same people you would always know. For your great great great grandmother cavewoman, there was no such thing as walking down the road past a stream of endless faces she didn't know. She knew everyone, and they knew her.

If you live in an even slightly populated area, you probably have this weird sensation each and every day. You walk through a busy city center and every other human being's face is a mystery to you. Who are they? You don't know and might never know. And who cares, right? You might even see the same person a few times in your area, but both of you will leave this earth after you're done and be none the wiser about each others' lives. Weird, isn't it?

Though humans are incredibly resilient and adaptable, you can begin to see how this might cause an incredible sense of alienation. People - in all their living, breathing, beautiful, infuriating, fascinating fullness - just fade into the background and become part of the noise of life. You go to a coffee shop, encounter three people in the line, another two at the counter, another one as you leave. You may chat and have a conversation with them, but they never stop being "background".

Is it any wonder that people feel so lonely in a world crawling with 7 billion people? Doesn't this explain why people stay at home, alone, making desperate online dating profiles while their neighbors do the same literally a few feet away from them in surrounding apartments?

How could you care much about your fellow human beings when, realistically speaking, you've never met any of them? Do the math quickly: if you only know, let's say, 200 people, that's only 0,000002% of the total world population. If you only speak and engage meaningfully to one of the hundreds of people you bump into today, the ratio is better but still vanishingly small. No wonder it's easy for us to watch the news where thousands of people die tragically and think, "meh".

Today, we're going to give our budding sense of awareness an empathic, human flavor. For some people, the following exercises will be the easiest of all in the book, for others it will feel completely bizarre and uncomfortable. But one thing's for sure, trying them out will open up new channels that were perhaps not open before.

For the first exercise, I'm going to ask you to try and take off the mask. We all walk around the world with a thin veneer made of good manners and disinterest and social conditioning. Of course, for the most part it probably should be there, but it pays to remind ourselves occasionally what's underneath it. Human beings! Nice ones!

Adjust the exercise depending on your regular routine. We've had some practice in turning our focus and awareness onto inanimate things in the environment and the contents of our own brains, now we'll turn that same spotlight onto other people.

Whoever you encounter today, do it openly, honestly and with full, unattached, non-judgmental, curious awareness. Be calm, alert and perfectly awake to what is unfolding in front of you - and human beings are really miraculous, when you look at them right (yes, even that weird guy sitting and talking to himself on the subway).

I'm not asking you to make lifelong friends with your irritating neighbor or fall in love with the guy at the cafe, although I guess I am heartily recommending that you become an "awareness slut".

When you talk to someone, really talk. Really listen. Make eye contact.

Be aware of the whole person who is standing in front of you - what magic did it take to carry them through their life until this point, to land right here, in front of you, as they are? What are they communicating, not just with words but with their whole being?

Really look at them - what do you see? Experience them fully just the same way you've practiced experiencing other sights and sounds fully. Notice how they make *you* feel. Notice what judgments spring up in your mind about them. Become aware of yourself, of them, and then that special space *between* you.

People who are "good with people" sometimes seem to be born with this skill already in tact. Just the same way someone else is skilled with a piano or a math theorem or a hacksaw, they seem to have an aptitude for all the moving parts of what makes people people. If you lack this skill, don't worry - as a human being it comes part of your built in software package, I promise! It just takes practice.

- Smile. Approach "strangers" with a feeling in your heart that they are not in fact strangers at all. Walk past a person in the street and make eye contact and smile the same way you would if you bumped into an old and dear friend. Hey, I'm not going to guarantee it will always end up well ...but on the other hand, it might.

- Kill small talk. When someone asks you how you are, tell them. You don't have to launch into a soliloquy about your antibiotic resistant toe fungus, but say something human and real and genuine.

- Don't let any encounter go by unnoticed. Acknowledge people, even if only in the smallest way. Don't plug in your literal or figurative earphones.

- Become aware of how you are presenting yourself to others. When you interact with people, what's your voice, posture and facial expression like? If an alien came out of space to watch you right at that moment and couldn't understand your language, what message would he assume you are sending to your fellow humanoid?

Day Fourteen: The Importance of Breath

Today, another simple exercise: breathing. Today, focus all your attention on your breathing. Is it fast and shallow at times? Are you holding it in a lot? Panting? Breathing from the stomach or the chest? Take a moment to really relish a few breaths when you can remember.

Day Fifteen: Fine Tuning a Genuine Sense of Empathy

You know what's useless? Tolerance. No concept in the world is so successful at promoting the exact kind of attitude and behavior it claims to rail against. When I hear "tolerance" I picture a cat I had as a child who would stoically endure the neighborhood kids dressing her up and forcing her to behave at tea parties. One look at her face said she wasn't exactly thrilled at having to wear a hat and sit at a plastic kiddie table, but, well, she *tolerated* it.

Not quite the picture of glowing compassion and empathy, is it?

Today, as an extension of yesterday's exercise, we'll try to foster a *real* sense of empathy for our fellow human beings. Not the kind of tolerance that has you saying passive aggressive things like, "No, no, that's fine, really, he's free to do whatever he wants! I don't agree myself, and I certainly would never do anything that boneheaded, of course, but he's more than welcome to do it if he wants to…"

Is anyone ever convinced by this kind of attitude? Instead of faux "tolerance", lets try today to develop a real *understanding* of other people. The exercise I'm going to suggest is quite simple, a little nutty sounding but very, very effective. I encourage you to really try with it, as just a few hours of this exercise *will* have tangible effects.

It goes thus: go out into the world, the busier and more densely populated the place, the better. Now, change your thought radio station and try to focus on the people you see in front of you. Allow your eyes to rest on anyone and focus on them for a bit. In your mind, say to yourself, *"there I am"* and for a moment, talk to yourself as though you are that person. I'm not advocating you push yourself into a weird psychosis, just bear with me for a second.

If you see a pretty girl with blue and grey hair and a frown, say to yourself "there I go with my blue and grey hair. I'm pretty. I have a frown." If you see a man carrying his son on his shoulders, tell yourself, "I'm carrying my son on my shoulders. I'm telling him to stop wriggling so much."

Keep this up, and try it out with as many different kinds of people as you can. The more different they are from you, the better. Talk to yourself about their appearances, their actions. If you like, you can start talking to yourself about their inner emotions and thoughts as well - although if you're a naturally more empathic person, you'll probably try to do this anyway.

What's the point of all this? It's not to turn *you* into the weird guy sitting on the subway talking to himself, I promise! But if you do it for long enough, something interesting will start to happen. You'll start to really *identify* with other people. Our language ordinarily emphasizes the differences between us quite strongly - you, me, him, her. But when you do an experiment and take those distinctions away, you give your brain the chance to see that actually, there really *is* a lot in common with you and the people around you. No tolerance necessary!

If you watch a child having a tantrum, and tell yourself, "there I am, being a big fat brat and making a nuisance of myself" you might give your brain the chance to remember that yes, you were in fact once a child and probably (absolutely) did the same thing. In fact, we were all once children. Look at the old lady who is tired and fed up with everything. Momentarily put yourself in her shoes and you'll have a thought many people don't allow themselves to have when it comes to very old people: that in time, you'll be in exactly the same place.

What this exercise does is teaches you real, felt empathy, not some lame sense of "tolerance" that you can wear like a badge. When you become mindful of everyone's shared humanity, of how similar we really are when it comes down to it, empathy is not something you have to endure like my poor childhood cat, it's just something that seems obvious and right to you.

Practice this exercise often enough and you will notice that you feel more in tune and connected with other people, that you may find it easier to communicate with them, understand them and make yourself understood. It might be easier to forgive them (or yourself!) and you might find your interactions suddenly become richer, deeper and more meaningful.

And maybe *then* you fall in love with the hot guy at the cafe, who am I to say.

The point is, congratulations, you have started to move your fellow human beings out of the zone of unawareness and "background" and into the zone where meaningful, empathetic interaction can take place.

Day Sixteen: Reflection

Today, an empty space. Clear away thoughts, reflect a little. What does it feel like to have "nothing"?

Day Seventeen: Formal Meditation

Typically when people think of meditation, it's formal meditation they're thinking of. And formal meditation is great. Sadly, the name doesn't imply that you can wear a ballgown and opera-length gloves when you do it (although, now that I think of it, you totally can do that if you want to) but it does imply that you're taking a very deliberate step to sit down and do something with conscious intention.

I personally find that more people have difficulty with formal rather than informal meditation. The truth is, formal meditation comes with a lot of "baggage". We all have preconceived ideas about what it should look like, all the religious and philosophical history behind the act, all the expectations and value judgments - you just sat down and crossed your legs, but you've really signed up for quite an elaborate process, haven't you?

Many gurus, teachers and know-it-all friends suggest starting a formal meditation practice first and then gradually incorporating informal activities throughout the rest of your day. Since I'm a little bit contrarian and like my living a little more loosey-goosey, my advice here would be to do the *opposite*. In fact, focus on opening those little awareness windows throughout the day and you won't have any need of a formal practice.

A formal practice may be a good thing to get going if you find that you respond well to structure, or have difficulty remembering to be more aware throughout the day. But once you can manage to maintain focus and relaxed awareness for longer and longer while sitting formally, gradually wean yourself off and instead turn to the real world - the best laboratory!

A good beginner's formal sitting meditation

- Find a place you know you won't be disturbed for a while, for a good 20 to 30 minutes. You can adjust the time according to your needs.

- Sit comfortably cross legged and rest your hands loosely. No need for a lotus position or awkward hand positions if these will only pull your attention away from focus in the moment.

- You don't need to close your eyes - although closing them does make it a bit easier. Gaze softly straight ahead if you like.

- Spend a few moments finding your breath first. Start to become aware of the air entering and leaving your nostrils, the rise and fall of your chest and the sensation and rhythm of breathing. Remember that you are not actively striving to control anything, only to observe and become aware.

- Once you feel a relaxed, alert sense of awareness on your breath, turn your thoughts outside yourself and become aware of what's going on with each of your senses. Acknowledge the sights, sounds, tastes, touch and other senses, such as the feeling of your weight pressing down into the floor, or the temperature around you. Feel the air literally touching the atoms that make up the surface of your skin. Dwell here for a bit.

- Lastly, turn your consciousness to your inner terrain and all the movements that are happening there. Observe calmly, not attaching to any one thought or feeling. Just like clouds come into the sky and then leave, watch thoughts appear and then float off again. Maintain awareness of the blue sky that persists underneath all the weather.

- When your mind wanders - when you get engrossed in a thought and start attaching strongly to it ("I'm doing this wrong! Ugh this is boring. I wonder what's for dinner. That cow was wrong about what she said the other day. Remember to be more aware! You're doing it wrong again. What's that smell dammit?") just remember to gently pull your awareness back again. There's no scolding yourself or forcing yourself to "think of nothing". No judgment, no grasping. Just be gently, calmly mindful. It doesn't matter if you lose focus a thousand times in a short 5 minute meditation. All that matters is that you bring your awareness back again. Know that whatever happens, it's all "grist for the mill". There is no way to fail. Your only job is to notice, and be awake in the present moment. Simple.

Some people like to have a regular daily formal meditation and find that this develops a sense of discipline and commitment that can be very sobering. I personally am not one of these people, but to each his own. If you're new to meditation, I believe a good goal to have is to slowly start finding real, organic moments of awareness in your "normal" life.

There isn't anything special or different about the awareness you're developing in formal meditation, and you can seriously whip out this state of mind whether you're washing dishes or yelling at a taxi driver about all the interesting ways you plan to kill his family if he doesn't get out of the way.

Day Eighteen: Reflect

In a sense, all of mindfulness is about "reflection"... when your spirit is calm and clear, you become still like the surface of a lake and can literally reflect what is happening around you. The more still your mind, the easier it becomes to accurately take in reality around you.

Today, either in a journal or any way that feels good for you, consider some of these questions to evaluate your "progress".

- How have you found the whole process in general?

- Have there been days that you haven't cared much about this stupid mindfulness business and given up? What was different about these days compared to the ones where you cared and took great effort?

- Have you noticed any difference in the way you are with other people?

- Are there any recurring thoughts that keep popping into your mind? What has your response been to those thoughts each time?

- What happens when you try not to judge or attach value and meaning to the things around you? Do you find the process scary? Boring? Strange? Freeing?

- What kind of thought traffic is common for you? If your mind was a TV station, what channels would play the most often?

- Do you have a goal for how you intend to finish this guide? Has your ego been holding onto a very specific outcome?

Day Nineteen: The Beautiful Ordinary

Probably because it would make the most boring commercial the world has ever seen, mindfulness is never sold as something that's just ...ordinary. The standard way to think about self-improvement is to imagine that when it happens, it looks markedly different from "normal life".

If you were ever tempted to pay to go on a special Buddhist retreat or mindfulness workshop, you might have felt pleased at all the "props": you had to drive somewhere special, maybe there were special people wearing exotic clothes, and everything was very magical and not at all ordinary. Your task then would be to try and see if you could remember how magical it all felt after you go home and get back to filing your tax forms and doing your laundry.

When we let go of the idea of wanting reality to be something that pleases us, when we are happy and brave enough to look at the world for what it is rather than what we wish it would be, we may notice something: it's kind of just OK.

Fostering a sense of tranquility in your heart and a spirit of non-attachment doesn't mean there aren't assholes in the world or that things don't break or get dirty or that there are no difficulties or moments of confusion or boredom. In fact, all of that pretty much stays exactly the same as it always was.

The difference is that by being mindful, we are in control of our response to it, and no matter what fleeting sensations occur in the external world (or the internal one for that matter!) nothing disturbs the deeper sense of calm we focus on. Today, try focus on accepting the massive, overwhelming sense of life's ordinariness.

Day Twenty: Self Compassion

Today, do a meditation where you look closely at yourself and turn your growing sense of acceptance inward. Are there things you can forgive yourself for? Things you've been holding onto?

Day Twenty One: We End ... at the Beginning

If you've reached the end of this book and feel as though you're still a totally newbie when it comes to mindfulness, congratulations! Seriously, the great thing about the present moment is that there's always a new one just around the corner. It's always the beginning. It's always *now*.

My hope is that in doing the 21-Day Mindfulness Challenge you've begun to develop your own sense for how mindfulness can create more peace, calm, acceptance and joy in your life. In fact, my hope is that this has *already* happened! Awareness of the present moment is a gift, but it's a gift that belongs to everyone, all the time.

The last challenge I will pose to you is this: given this endlessly refreshing present moment, given how amazing it is to always be at the beginning, to always have a fresh chance to make a new start, what will you do? What ways can you honor the moment that lives at the very end of this sentence...?

Made in the USA
Middletown, DE
04 March 2017